BAD OMENS

JESSICA DRAKE-THOMAS

Bad Omens

Jessica Drake-Thomas

QUERENCIA

Querencia Press, LLC
Chicago, Illinois

QUERENCIA PRESS

LIBRARY OF CONGRESS CATALOGING-IN-PUBLICATION DATA

ISBN 978 1 959118 09 1

www.querenciapress.com

First Published in 2022

Querencia Press, LLC
Chicago IL

Printed & Bound in the United States of America

"This anger endangers one's hold over convention. It places one beyond the pale. It announces one's emerging self... (This anger) expresses love and an unwillingness to accept anything but love in return."

–María Lugones

*For my mother, who has always encouraged both the writer
and the reader in me.*

CONTENTS

SPEAK TO ME

as if I'm covered in blood:
a crimson dress
of sacrifice's incarnadine,
or don't speak
at all.
Bring me a gift—
mouthful of sour cherries,
black toad,
smooth rune-stones.
In return,
the knowledge
you've been denied
by those who kneel
on cold, hard floors.

WHEN MY FEET TOUCHED DARK SOIL,

flowers sprang up.

Why does the sight
of meadowsweet
make me sad?

It reminds me of who I once was,
the power I had,

under the face of the sun.

When I fell, I did not fall alone,
now I suffer in the dark,
my sadness, a bitter fruit,
lodged in my throat.

HELHEST (Hel's Horse)

I accept you, three-legged and rotting,
cursed, first-in-the-grave. Sacrificial gift-horse,
your abnormal hoofbeats, clatter in the night,
the death-bell,
warning them of our coming

We will collect ghosts together.
Me, a two-faced goddess, and
you, my heart,
my blue one—bloodless, best.

UNTITLED

When Eve ate the apple, she was granted knowledge.
Why should I feel guilty about that? In the same place,
I'd do the same thing.

They've burned women
for knowing less.

Here's what I know—there's power
in this stone, that fits in the palm of my hand.
The feel of the grass beneath my feet.
There's magic in simple things—

In being able to make choices,
give consent.

The apple was a gift, not a curse.
Power, over those who would possess my body,
though they fear me, my voice.

I don't want to be a sheep—
I want to be a scorpion,
for my aim to be true.

THE LOVED ONES

The family stands together around their lost one,
swathed in black crepe
mourning garb, faces static.
She lies there, decaying in front of them,
heaped in flowers,
a white casket.
Her cheek's bruised like bad fruit.
She looks so peaceful,
like a stolen bride in a story,
a changeling, taken by the fae queen for her own.
In their dreams, she contacts her family,
lets them know she's well, beneath the hill.
> They watch as she walks away, into the afterglow.
> *Who is sleeping*, the loved ones wonder—
> *who is awake?*

DESCENT

Feet on the bottom, staring up through blue water,
sunbeams. When I fell, I forgot to come back up.

The first time these mortal eyes beheld Death, I saw she
was beautiful. She reached out, her palm caressing my
cheek. She whispered to me—

Pale hands, pull me upwards. Rebirth, sound—my mother's
voice.

BAD BROOD

Part of being a witch is giving
the dark shadow that follows you
a name
so it may live.

What do you want?
Speak your truth.
Let it manifest from your lungs
like locusts.

READING IN THE BATH

Steam warps the pages of my paperback copy of the
Kalevala.
I'm flushed pink, skin smoldering, hair curling over
my shoulder blades, the high mountains,
knees rising to form islands
of the scarred land of my body,
surrounded by the constant abuse of the moon's tides.

I'm a witch, born out of generations of god-fearing people
who bent their heads and their knees.

I am a force of my own design.

Seabirds circle my head, lay three eggs on the nest of my
kneecap.
A gold one, a freckled one, and a black one—
Sun, stars, and the dark, good earth.

I carve out rivers from the dirt, shape bowls for oceans,
crack the shells to light up the sky,
weave spells into sacred forests,
fill them with ghosts,
then rinse my hair.

BOOK OF THE DEAD

I think a lot about the postmortem photographs that Grace discovers in the attic in *The Others*. They're in an ornate black book, held shut with golden clasps, each page a window into a death. People in Victorian mourning attire, heads lolling as if thrown down by a deadly nocturne. The color faded out of them. Eyelids pressed closed. Mouths pinned shut.

Grace called them *macabre*—the word was dark coffee and spice in my mouth. At thirteen years old, I wanted to put it on. Let it pool in my hands like velvet, wrapping it around myself like a cloak, disappearing into the fog.

RUSSIAN DOLL

I'm opening up, you see:
I unzip my skin so another
version of me steps out.
Each one worse
than the one before.

None are real,
these women that you see,
they're mirrors.

For a little while,
I can be whoever
you want me to, but

I'm the woman who dreams vividly
of burning to death.
I wake suddenly, then
catch fire, crackling.
I rise from my own ashes.

When I open my eyes,
I'm still on fire, the shadows
casting strangely on the walls.

VENA AMORIS

In your eyes I was reborn.
I wanted to be the woman you imagined, but
I'm a trigger, begging to be pulled.
My kiss is a shot in the dark,
a cold barrel, pressed
against your teeth.

Like a siren song, I will drag you
six feet under,
into the dark dirt of my affection.
My love line slants
downward,
plunging like a bird
through the sky.

COLD MOON RITUAL

These dark wells draw dark water,
and I'm drowning in them.
I've filled them with shadows,
set down offerings on ground
saturated with sorrow—
here's a handful of gravedirt,
a songbird stuck with pins,
here's the cold moon,
hanging in the sky—
a round, silver coin for my pocket,
and a trail of footprints,
leading off into the darkness.
Someone's crying, softly.
Do not follow that trail.
The marsh is an open mouth,
able to swallow a person whole.
I want everything to go back
to how it was before she died,
press my fingers to wood—
unlock my chest,
take out my heart
of dark blue meat,
feed it to her starving ghost.

DARK ALCHEMY

It's stunningly clear—/he's rushing off to sleep with
someone else./ I can tell by the hasty, distracted kiss,/ how
he hides his phone./ I'm Twombley's *The Rose V*—/blooming
blood-dark & dripping,/ a *nouveau séance* on my phone,/
crosslegged on the floor, googling/ black magic rituals with
my dog.// Rage is the eye of the storm: utter calm.// The
mirror's a portal into the Otherworld,/ stare deeply into the
dark pools, my eyes—/prick my finger with a pin, pressing
wound/ to cool, wax-spattered glass./ Speak her name.
Speak it again—/A low rumble, as my dog growls./ In my
reflection,/ I see the outline of her, her shadow/detaching
from the others in the room./ She stands behind me—/her
knotty hair, her wet shift clinging to her skin./ Light
gleams/ in the dark alchemy of our eyes./ I smell blood, ash./
Feel her cold fingers on my neck./ I speak our name, again:
witch./ Whose blood do I smell?/ Whose voice do I hear?/
Both, mingling as/ everything fades out.

When I wake, the sun is coming up,/ a blue desert dawn—
/I've got strange symbols/ drawn in pen on my arm.

THE DEVIL//THE LOVERS

Trailing kisses along your neck,
candlelight flickering across our skin.
Watch as the shadows dance.

Darling, you're shaking,
soft clink of chain-links
arms, legs, fingers, locking,
binding us, forever—

Darkling, Listen:
you're the only
demon on my back,

curl your curved horns
beneath my chin

my heart beats here,
petrichor in grave-dirt.

BLOOD OATH

We'll do this in the moon-bright
when the light is silver,
like the necklace you gave me.

One prick above the clavicle, lower your lips,
press a kiss,
drink the drop of blood wine
to seal our oath.
For we are a rope with two ends,
a double-edged sword.

You may try to hang me
with rope that binds us,
then hang yourself, instead.

FENRIR

He stands in the Western door—
creature of the night,
hungers for the sun
to fill his belly.

A chain, crafted of whispers,
holds him.
His tail wraps around
my ankle.
My fingers grasp his fur,
I see
a dog's eye, a god's eye—
a full silver moon.
As his teeth dig into my skin—
all the priests
throw their heads back,
howl.

THE WOLVES

When my heart beat
against bone,
I dreamed of hiding
among silent pines.

I was always hungry, when
I belonged to him—

his blood-spackled grin,
feral eyes fixing me in place.

Until the night
filled with snap of bone and sinew;
clack of teeth.

He curled up and slept:
a satiated Saturn,
saving me for seconds.

I left,
locking the door behind me.

Branches grabbed my hair
as I ran through the snow
toward amber lights,
feet blue as a dead bride.

When they cut away the frostbite
to keep me alive,
there was so much blood—

Unlike the moon,
I will never be whole,
but that's okay.

Sometimes I wake
in the middle of the night
to the sound of
wolves howling
inside me.
The shadows shift
in the corners of the room
moving with predatory grace,
eyes of pale fire—

ANATOMICAL VENUS

He likes a woman
who's pale & pliant as wax.
She lays back,
cupid's bow lips closed
in perfect, gentle repose.

Real golden locks
in perfect waves,
spilling across the silk pillow.
Pearls at her neck,

              eyes glazed blue.

She can be opened up
like a cabinet,

          her organs removed,
put back together,   a puzzle
that needn't be solved.
Her face can be pulled back
to reveal   a staring skull, with eyes still in,
teeth, bared

                 like a wolf.

THE ASH TREE

I thought it would bring me joy
to fall in love.
It has not.

I stand alone,
ash with deep roots,
strong branches,
existing for the smell
of rain hitting dry earth.

I've weathered
so many lies,
people carving
their initials
into my skin,
then leaving.

Who knew that the touch of a man
was so ruinous to woman?
From the way they talk,
you'd think there'd be marks.

It's not her fault, it's the man's.
That he should believe
knowledge of any kind
makes her less than she was before.

We who have two natures know—
It's best to keep our secrets,
to remain unknown.
Yet we still want love.
Women have contorted themselves for it
with corsets and heels,
poisoned themselves
with belladonna eyedrops,
when all he wants is a body.

Let me tell you what I've learned—
Don't fall for a creature who dissembles,
who knows all the right things to say.
Don't fall in love with a person
whose touch is your doom.

OBSESSIONS WITH TRAGEDIES

The meeting of morbid minds,
two blonde girls wearing red lipstick,
winged black eyeliner,
spelling out messages
with a plastic planchette.

She loved hers glamorous,
hard glitter & sparkle—
The Titanic, James Dean's car-wreck,
picture-perfect suicide of Evelyn McHale.

My love's macabre,
blood & teeth—Ed Gein's lampshade,
H.H. Holmes's murder palace,
husband's heart in Mary Shelley's pocket.

Last time she called, upset about her coworker:
He reached across the table, took my hand in his,
his wedding ring, cold against my skin.

There are no good men, I replied, *only good liars.*
I believe in love, I just can't find it, she said.
Now she's gone, I wonder
how I didn't see this coming.
The storyteller, wanting all pieces,
only holding fragments—beginning, epilogue.

What caused her to spiral like that?

What dark nautilus lurks at its calcified heart?

I'm pressing my fingers to planchette:
no answer this time.
It's there, glistening like an oil slick;
a knot I'll never unsnarl

closing off my throat,
binding me to her
silent, pale-haired ghost.

TWO OF SWORDS

Lost in the unending night
of his gaze,
I believed him when
he whispered in my ear.
I let his chaos close around me
like a fist.

Ensconced in this void,
I breathed little—lived on dreams as
white flowers bloomed in my belly, thinking
of lips, painted by vanilla vodka, a violin's curve,
a world of strange and beautiful magnets,
governed by balance.

He was the king on a toppled chair,
his tumbledown tower at his feet.

He gave me an orchard of rotting fruit, and
seven years of bad luck
because I didn't love him.

Blindfolded, I unsheathed my swords.
The hand opened, a flat palm, pale in the twilight.
    Alone, I walked the shoreline, strewn with wreckage,
    through the gate to the garden of bones.

I had a nightmare
that you asked me
to marry you,
forcing a false diamond
ring onto my finger,
& it broke,
swelling, purple.
The ring was stuck.

You paraded me around.
I had to show everyone,
pretending my finger
wasn't broken,
despite the obvious.

I'm all too aware
of the noose you
slipped around my neck
while I was sleeping,

how you tugged
with false promises
nearly snapping my
head from my neck.

When I wake, I can't believe
how wonderfully free
I am.

PUT THE BONES BACK

I associate Christianity with violence because the man who
raised me
wielded his god like a knife.
It's how I protect myself. *Jesus has forgiven me*, he said.
...but I haven't, I replied, remembering everything, while
he neatly excised me from what happened—
I'm the object, the mutilated child,
sacrificed again and again for my father's well-being.
I think of the way his mask would appear in church,
then go away the second the car doors slammed shut.
The fabric of the universe depends on who's looking,
whether one sees the face in the witch's window,
or the blurred reflection of a bird, a fault in the picture.
Just because someone's colorblind doesn't mean that blue
doesn't exist.
Just because a priest grants absolution doesn't mean the
pain caused is gone.
I sat with a black beeswax candle, staring into the flame,
trying to banish all this anger within me,
and I failed.
I endured people telling me
what a sweet, kind man my father was,
knowing the truth—I've been the one haunting this story,
walking the dark halls late at night.
In the Ancient Ram Inn, they found the bones of children,
buried beneath one of the fireplaces.
Rusty knives, too. Then, they put the bones back,

to appease our angry spirits.

SEA-WITCH

I'm haunted by his eyes,
glowing white moons
in the rotten sky of his face.

He took my voice,
made me cower in the corner.
I know what pain is, fear.

I bled him out
to feed my spells.
When you're willing
to feed something blood,
eventually it thrives.

While he floats backwards
in the current, the fish pick
his bones clean.

It's quiet here,
in my house of bones.
My hair floats on the current
like anemones, sea-grass.

I close the bright stars
of my eyes. Satiated,
I sleep, sinking into the deep.

Dark Lady, Poison Mama,
they stoned all your crows.
Your midnight flock
lies broken on the ground.
Doomed men will tempt
a goddess' anger
to avoid their fate, then seal it.

You spill salt as you walk
leaving spoiled earth
in your wake.

You are the bad omen
washing dead men's clothes
in the cold lake.

The black depths will take
them for what they did.
As they breathe their last,
ravens rise into the air.

BELLADONNA

It is of a cold nature; in some it causeth sleep; in others madness, and, shortly after, death. — Culpeper's Complete Herbal

Atropos is the blind Fate
who snips the thread
of human lives
with her silver scissors,   ending them.
While her two sisters
weave & create,
she completes.
This ancient goddess
is *Atropa Belladonna's*
namesake. She's been served
to whole armies in cups of wine,
decimating their ranks.
She's been sold
as women's perfume,
to get rid of abusive husbands.
Though she's small,
her implications are large.
She's one of the most
destructive herbs in creation.
She's a black hole,
a monster with a gaping maw,
hidden in the guise
of a beautiful flower.

OCCLUSION

When people stand next to each other,
something's hidden.
A closed fist, behind the back;
a hand in her pocket;
a smirk, when her face is turned away;
a doubtful glance;
a green eye.

What's in her hand, pray tell—
deadly nightshade berries? A spell?
An orchid? A cameo pin?

What lingers behind her dreadful smile?

The demimonde, crowding around her,
demanding she follow the rules,
will never know;

she owes them
nothing.

When he stands
in front of the girl
to steal away
the crow in her hands,
snapping its neck,

to put the fear of his god into
the old spirit looking out her eyes,
to put out the fire
in her heart,

to deny her wisdom,

to quell the spells,
pouring from her lips,

he fears her—
she knows this.

THE EMPRESS REVERSED

There's a brisk trade for photographs of dead women[1],
you know—
men like their women silent, passive.
Weak, soft as a kitten.

They cannot stand a mad woman,
who speaks in tongues,
knows secrets.

A woman is only as good
as those she trusts.

Her blue lips gape—

spiders come crawling
out of her mouth
her eyes go black.

She lifts up off her feet,
head thrown back.
There's a demon beneath her skin,
scratching to get loose.

Like this pattern she's dragging her nails down—
yellow wallpaper, purple orchids,
death cap mushrooms,
a woman slipping out
of her body, her prison.

---

[1] *Penny Dreadful*, Season One, Episode Seven.

Have you seen the signs? They're in
patterns that birds make in the sky,
footprints marking the road she took,
veins in leaves, the way the cards fall,
how the moon occludes itself.

Who is this? Who's it from?
The cold woman, with eyes of blue flame.
The prints end, trail runs dry.
Your questions do not.

THREE OF SWORDS

In the Middle Ages, they'd press three iron nails
into the heart of a bull & throw it on the fire.
Correspondences in magic mean
this would burn the witch.

One time, I found a poppet
in an antique store.
She wore a purple cotton dress,
woven straw hat. Her face was completely
burned off, charred stuffing spilling out.

What was unnerving was the time & care
spent making her—painstakingly:
tiny, perfect stitches, a calm hand.

Even love can't bind love. But intention can.

I'm reading a book that smells of tattoo ink, thinking of
needles, a permanent bird flying across
                                    a wrist.

OPHIOPHAGY

All the world's on fire; I knew this
was coming in September. Heralded by
vivid dreams of being so sick
I couldn't move. Another of a large
black & gold snake, hunting me.

I know it's going to be bad.
Instead, I sprinkle my hair & vinegar
to rid the yard of the snake from my dream.

We don't want your
witchcraft, my sister says.
We want scientific facts.

I'm using my craft to locate
boundaries: where real & unreal touch.

Scents will warn away the snake,
this good-dreams poppet,
tucked beneath my pillow
will keep the dreams away.

I may be asleep when
disaster arrives, but
I'll dream of dandelion pie & stars

Nature threw back her head and howled,
dark cloud pouring from her lips.
The folk thought they were unbeatable,
their magic would save them.
They died the straw death,
falling like rain.

No help came.

There were no bright swords,
no bravery—just death.

Hungry ghosts fed on ample flesh.
Black birds flew over
the corpses,
eating the entrails.
All that was left
was silence,
hanging over an abattoir.

Nature smiled with her sharp teeth,
her feral eyes feasting on
the destruction
that she wrought.

The sun and the moon
still ran from the wolves,
the tides continued,
and the mountains still
rose above the quiet land.

I've two faces, one always hidden,
the other grinning like a skull.
I'm always going down in flames,
singing as I burn out like stars
because I'm a broken, shunned creature,
even though the road beneath my feet
is cracked like my teeth.
I'll eat the golden apple, wear the darkling crown,
let the wolves loose, then
betray whatever heaven
where the godly go to rest
because even stilled, my dark heart
is always true.

LA FÉE VERTE

I.

It was the day I fell apart,
walking home, looking at the bright sky,
avoiding cacti near the cracked sidewalk,
knowing that the fall was coming.
I was wearing a skull print blouse,
green mechanic's jacket—the one with pockets big enough
for paperbacks.
I'd left school early, gone to 4th Avenue,
went to visit my tarot reader.

She pulled the Tower,
harbinger of melt-downs
at the center of the spread.

I clinked my ring-stone against a chain-link fence
as I walked by. Thinking of green.

II.

One time I drank absinthe
in a Russian-themed bar in New Orleans.
The liquor was milky chartreuse.
I searched for the green fairy,
found nothing but astringent anis,
butterfly kisses over a Ouija board.
Nothing answered. No ghosts. No demons
from the unseelie court.

III.

Victorian era women liked the way their green silk gowns
shimmered in new electric lighting.
Then people started getting sick—
from the Arsenic used to make the color.

IV.

Matilda Scheurer was nineteen.
Her job at the factory was to
powder floral headpieces with a green dye,
until she vomited green, and
her nails and eyes were green
and the last thing she said she could see: green,

V.

like absinthe. So the day—the one where
I had a meltdown, I picked up
a bottle for old time's sake. To search for
the green fairy who
never arrives.

VI.

In the mirror, I stare into my eyes—
not hazel, but dark jade,
green seeps through my pores
glows out of my eyes.
My pupils dilate, trying to cover it up;
it always bleeds through.

VII.

Instead, this warm, sugar-soft feeling
which tricks me
into liking myself
for a little while.
I love that that which
kills me, makes me
ill the next day.

VIII.

I turn over the top
card to find the Tower—
silver ring around the bottle,
ashes, ashes,
all falls down,
foundations crack
like skulls and bones,
and I take another sip.

IX.

The green fairy raises her head,
opens her sage wings wide.
Her eyes glitter.
When she opens her mouth,
green comes spilling out.
She opens her arms,
she is me, I am her—
I step into her killing embrace.

UNKNOWN COUNTRY

Headlights—they remind me of Christmases long ago,
lines of red, white.
People passing each other in the night.
Wheels on wet pavement. The rain on the windshield.

We're all in existence, passing on our way to elsewhere.
There's more than is dreamed in any philosophy,
the universe stretches out and—
sometimes, we crash, broken glass hitting the ground like
rain.

Here's an open window
to something else.
Touch the veil, peel it back
to find the ink and the black.

This is a meeting place
where the glow of the sunset
was blocked out
by the black trees.

The meeting of two
who had good intentions,
the indelible mark
on this land,
a hallow.

THE BONE THIEF

When I was studying art at Tulane,
my professors told stories
about a past student, dedicated to her craft.
She nailed meat to a large wooden cross,
left it in the sculpture studio over the weekend.
By Monday morning, it was rancid.
She'd go to Holt Cemetery,
the only one in the city with ground burials—
the graves were open, since the ground's so wet, caskets
float up.
One day, she opened her art locker, bones fell out—
a skull & baby's dirty dress,
ribcage still tucked lovingly inside.

I often find myself
carrying stories, wondering
what the endings were;

I know what the dead are like
when disturbed.

How are you associated with the hospital? the investigator
asks,
during an investigation in Linda Vista Hospital.
We're not dead, the voice says on the recorder, clear as
window glass:
We're not dead.

1466 COMMONWEALTH AVENUE

Not a smudge on a photograph nor a silk stocking
pulled from the painted lips of a false medium—
Sometimes, people go looking,
sometimes, they find you.
When they do, they make themselves known.

There was the Revolutionary War soldier,
whose throat had been shot away,
who would sit in my desk chair,
his coughing like dry leaves.

& the woman who was wrapped in
a dirty gray shroud, hair
slick with mud.

I wasn't able to ignore her
when she'd sit on my bed, running her fingers
over my cheek, whispering into the dark:
Can you see? She can feel my touch.

Voices unheard
by human ears for almost a century,
the others would whisper—

They were happy, while my heart
pounded against my sternum, a locked door.

They're still there in that apartment on Commonwealth
Avenue:
fish, in an aquarium, confetti, on the air.
They'll still be there after I'm dead.

One night, I dreamed I was back,
sunlight poured through the windows,
they were all crowding in the corners
like shadows, waiting for my return.

DARK CANTICLE

When the shadows
open their eyes
and whisper back,

when the black bird
flies into the window,
leaving behind a red mark—

press your ear to
the cold wood.
Listen for the knock
beneath the floorboards.

When you call out
into the void,
begging for release,
you will receive
your answer.

My blue one,
in your gray coat,
with your salt-flecked hair—
you travel the world
under false faces,
walking seen and unseen.

When you dream,
you are in
my arms.
I feed you

golden apples.
that taste of
sunlight and whispers.

We sit beneath the ash tree,
its roots curl around you
as you sleep,
pulling you down,
into the dark dirt.

DEATH

Your eyes will open like roses
blooming to reveal
that you are not alone.
You see, I come after.
I'm the real patron of lost causes.

I'll lift you
out of the hole the
priests put you in.
There are no tears,
no ashes, here,
take this silver necklace,
wrap it around your neck.

Come, ride this pale horse
to the ending of this world—
the veil between,
my black tattered cloak
around your shoulders.

OUROBOUROS

My bare feet broke
crust of new-fallen snow.

I pulled back my hood
to reveal my two faces:
my toothy skull grins,
turn my head—
pale lips twist downward.

Golden-eyed snake, he
wrapped around me,
sinuous body trapping my arms.

I was pressed to the earth,
tasted iron, snow.

Cold slithering scales,
the one who waits
to swallow the world.

There's no apology
he could make—
I was like a starving child,
on my knees, begging for release.

QUEEN OF THE CROSSROADS

Your sacrifice will rebound. Go on,
tuck me down in the ground,
I'll rise again, same old spirit—

fresh crosses on my palms
when I wake.

Horseman, witch,
bad omen in the flesh—

eyes of glass, eyes of glass,
mouth of sharp teeth,

devourer of hearts,
whole & sweet.

NOTES ON PREVIOUS PUBLICATONS

The poems in this book have appeared in:

RESURRECTION Magazine

Terse Journal

Corvid Queen

Rogue Agent

Final Cut Zine

PVSSYMAGIC

NOTES

WHEN MY FEET TOUCHED DARK SOIL: Based on the story of Blodeuwedd, whose name in Welsh means "flower faced." With her lover, she murdered her husband. In witchcraft, Meadowsweet is used in love spells.

HELHEST: The horse that the Norse goddess Hel rides is three-legged because when the Norse would sacrifice a horse on a funeral pyre, they would remove one of the legs, so the horse would remain in the grave.

READING IN THE BATH: Based on the creation of the world, as per the Finnish epic story, *The Kalevala*.

BOOK OF THE DEAD: Based on the 2001 movie, *The Others*.

VENA AMORIS: Latin for the love line or vein in palmistry.

THE DEVIL/THE LOVERS: Plays with line from John Keats's "Ode to a Nightingale": "Darkling, I listen; and for many a time I have been half in love with easeful Death."

BLOOD OATH: Draws from a scene in Marion Zimmer Bradley's *The Mists of Avalon*.

FENRIR: Poem inspired from a line in *Vikings,* during the Siege of Paris, when Floki says: "The wolf stands by the Western door. We will all die."

ANATOMICAL VENUS: Written following reading a 2016 article in *The Guardian* by Zoe Williams, titled "Cadavers in Pearls: Meet the Anatomical Venus."

SEA WITCH: Written following reading Sabrina Orah Mark's article "The Silence of Witches" in *The Paris Review*.

OPHIOPHAGY: Final line is a reference to Shirley Jackson's novel, *We Have Always Lived in the Castle*.

I'VE TWO FACES, ONE ALWAYS HIDDEN: "I'm a broken shunned creature" is a reference to *Penny Dreadful*.

LA FÉE VERTE: Makes reference to "Sheele's Green: The Color of Fake Foliage and Death" by Katy Kelleher in *The Paris Review*.

UNKNOWN COUNTRY: Makes reference to Shakespeare's *Hamlet*.

HERE'S AN OPEN WINDOW: Makes reference to Season Two of *Hellier*.

THE BONE THIEF: Makes reference to the Linda Vista investigation done by APRA Paranormal.

DARK CANTICLE: Based off the 2016 movie, *A Dark Song*.

ACKNOWLEDGEMENTS

I wrote this book in my pajamas, in bed, during 2020. While the world outside was chaos, I soothed myself with witchcraft and myth in my cocoon of blankets, propped up against pillows while binge-watching *Supernatural, Penny Dreadful,* and *Vikings.*

Thanks to Emily Perkovich and Querencia Press, who saw the promise in this book. After many, many rejections, I'm glad to know that *Bad Omens* ended up in your good hands.

Special thanks go to my mother, to whom this book is dedicated. You have always encouraged me to follow my passions, especially as a reader and writer. A few years ago, you sat me down and told me to do the thing that I needed to. This book certainly wouldn't have existed without your support. Thank you.

Thanks to my support system: Elizabeth, Alexa, Christine, Kendall, Edison, and Nick. You all make me feel so loved and supported.

Thanks to my teachers at the University of Wisconsin Milwaukee, particularly Rebecca Dunham and Mauricio Kilwaen-Guevara, in whose workshop classes I produced several of the poems in this book. Additional thanks to Gwynne Kennedy, in whose Gender and Anger class I read feminist texts that provided inspiration for many poems in this book.

Many thanks to Lindsay Lusby for your keen editorial advice on a very early draft of this book.